Clevedon Pier

First published in 1981
by Redcliffe Press Ltd.,
14 Dowry Square, Bristol

ISBN 0 905459 24 5

Printed by Burleigh Ltd, Bristol

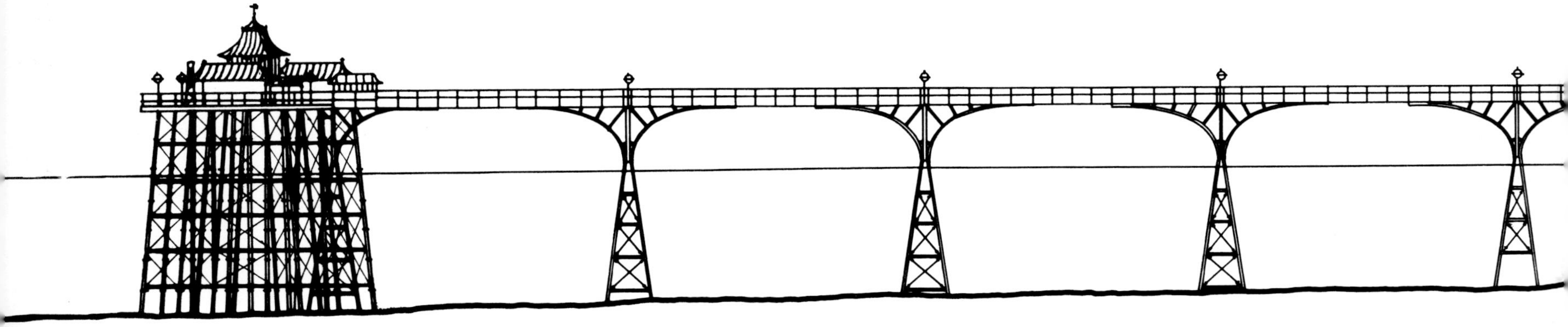

Clevedon Pier

by Keith Mallory

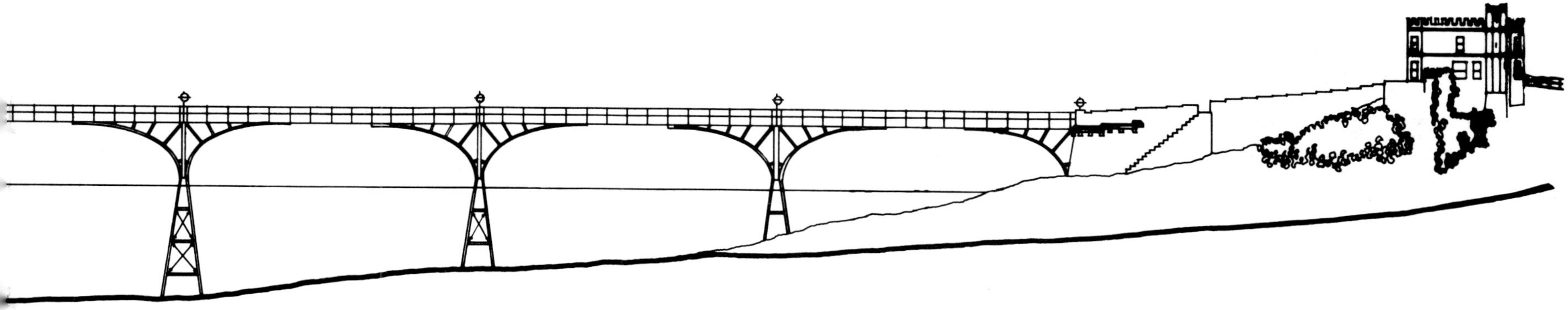

Preface

My personal interest in Clevedon and its pier originated with a survey of the pier which I carried out in the summer of 1967 with John Rayner. At that time the pier was little known outside Clevedon but, since its partial collapse during structural tests being carried out for insurance purposes in 1970, there has developed a growing national interest in seaside piers generally and in the future of Clevedon Pier in particular. No significant maintenance work has been carried out since its collapse and there is no doubt that the pier has been allowed to deteriorate badly over the last ten years. Following a long and detailed Public Inquiry in March 1980 the present owners, Woodspring District Council, were however refused permission to demolish the pier by the Secretary of State, Michael Heseltine, whose Inspector's Report referred to its 'unique' and 'delicate appearance'. Clevedon Pier Preservation Trust and Clevedon Pier Technical Group, both leading objectors at the Inquiry, are now negotiating with Woodspring District Council in order to obtain a lease of the pier and commence the now desperately needed restoration work. This book attempts to draw attention to the importance of the pier, both nationally and locally, and the overwhelming evidence in support of this restoration.

I am very grateful to John Rayner for permission to use the photographs and drawings which were prepared during our original survey, to my wife Cheryl who has helped with the research, and to the members of the Trust who have worked with me in preparing the book: Michael Allman, Frank Benatt, John Haden, Brian Hayward and Richard Pelter. Lady Elton, a leading member of the Trust for many years, has been particularly helpful and generous both in giving access to her own research on the subject and to the archives at Clevedon Court and also in giving advice during the preparation of the work. I am also grateful to the many other people and organisations who have helped with information and illustrations with special thanks to Victor Smith and Paul Canterell of the *South Avon Mercury*, former Town Surveyor John Topham, George Bees for his personal recollections, photographers Brian Middlehurst and Phillip Theobald, and finally but not least Sally Hook who typed the manuscript.

Keith Mallory
Clevedon May 1981

Contents

Long live Clevedon as a complete town, which
it would not be if it ever lost its Pier.

Sir John Betjeman, March 28, 1969

Marginal numbers in bold refer to main body of illustrations

On Easter Monday 1869 Clevedon, a small seaside town on the Bristol Channel, was
the scene of a spectacular public celebration. The town was decorated with
triumphal arches of evergreen branches, flags were flying, bands played and the crowds
cheered for what *The Clevedon Mercury* described at the time as 'the greatest gala day
Clevedon has ever experienced . . . the commencement of better times for our fair 5
Clevedon'.

The event, illustrated in *The London Illustrated News*, was the opening of Clevedon's
wrought iron pier and it marked a remarkable act of faith by the local businessmen of
this small town. Over one hundred years later the pier is still standing and, although in
need of repair, is a constant reminder of the confidence and ingenuity of the generation
which produced it.

Some seventy-five piers were constructed in the heyday of pier construction, the
period 1850–1900, and Clevedon Pier is arguably the most elegant and significant of the
fifty or so that remain.[1] Designed by Grover and Ward in 1867 it typifies the simplicity
and inventiveness of the best of nineteenth century engineering but it is also an
important and integral part of the town's topography. Providing a point of integration 1
between townscape and seascape it stretches into the channel from the base of a small
rocky promontory in an almost inevitable way and the town, curved and raked behind
it like like an auditorium, focuses on the pier from all points. It is the pier which draws
together the various nineteenth century features of the town and recreates the atmos-
phere of the English seaside town as it must have been in Victorian times. 62–6

1. See Appendix 1 for a list of the remaining piers.

The seaside town as a social focal point originated with the discovery in 1626 of a 'medical spring' in Scarborough, Yorkshire, but it was not until the end of the century that this was exploited. At that time Bath had already undergone a re-birth as the spa waters of Roman colonialists were rediscovered. Taking the waters had become socially acceptable and a lucrative business had grown up around it.

The sea was still, as Trevelyan aptly states, the Englishman's common, his fishpond, his battleground, his road and his heritage. It took several years for medical opinion to swing in favour of the practice of sea-water bathing and drinking and for the spiritual refreshment of either seas or mountains to be appreciated. By 1735, however, Scarborough was firmly established as a 'watering place' as we know from a painting by John Setterington, in the British Museum, which depicts a bathing scene some 200 years ago. The bathers, male and female, are completely naked. In the background are the everyday sights of a small harbour, fishing boats and barques, forming an invigorating contrast to the clammy pump rooms of the inland spas. Brighton was to become popular much later but the royal patronage by the Prince Regent produced a spectacular growth. Its famous Pavilion, designed by John Nash in a caricature of oriental architecture, was started in 1784 and set the style of seaside architecture for the next 100 years.[2]

2. Nash's pavilion made extensive use of cast iron for both structural and decorative elements. Until the use of coke for smelting in 1747 iron had been produced by elementary methods and used in building mainly for tensile members, tie bars and chains, and for wrought iron. By 1779 the first cast iron bridge was being built at Coalbrookdale by Abraham Darby.

By the early nineteenth century, children had begun to accompany their parents but it was the advent of cheap mass transport with the railways which finally opened up the seaside holiday to the new middle classes. The period 1850–1900 consequently saw a boom in the development of seaside towns although the seaside pier, as we know it, arrived in this context almost by chance.

The first pier to be used as a pleasure pier is generally accepted as being the Brighton Chain Pier, built in 1823 primarily as a landing point for the Brighton–Dieppe packets. It became sufficiently popular with visitors as a promenade to suggest that piers could be financially attractive in other seaside towns. Visitors could have all the pleasure of the sea, without the expense or discomfort of a voyage, as the *Visitors Guide to Clevedon* was to claim in 1890 in describing its pier as 'a favourite promenade with visitors . . . they can derive all the salutary advantages of the pure sea air without any risk of the dreaded nausea so often induced by being tossed upon its wavey surface'.

A pier became an essential amenity for any fashionable resort. By the mid-nineteenth century Clevedon was just such a resort, having grown rapidly from a population of only 334 in 1800. Its natural beauty had already been noted and it was mentioned in the *History and Antiquities of the County of Somerset* of 1791. Four years later the poet Coleridge was to spend his honeymoon in Clevedon which he describes as his 'Valley of Seclusion' with 'the sea's faint murmur' and landscape that 'refresh'd the eye'.

By the time of the publication in 1829 of John Rutter's *The Clevedon Guide*, something like forty new villas had been constructed around the town and by 1831 there was a population of 1147. This growth continued and was fed by the increasing demand from the nearby cities of Bristol and Bath. It took place within a structure of picturesque walks and open spaces planned by the local landowners, the Elton family, and the result was a townscape which appealed to a literate middle class now immersed in the Romantic Movement.[3] In 1847 the railway arrived, dramatically increasing the

3. See Curl 'A Victorian Coastal Arcadia'.

number of visitors and when the 1856 edition of Chilcott's *Clevedon New Guide* was published Wason's Royal Hotel had been constructed as well as hot and cold baths
near the water's edge. Several bathing machines were available for open sea-bathing. 7
Chilcott wrote in the introduction to his guide that 'the celebrity which Clevedon has obtained as a watering place, the rapid increase of its buildings, the beauty and variety of its scenery, walks, and rides together with the purity and salubrity of the air, have occasioned the publication of this little Guide'.

The construction of a pier was almost inevitable. Chilcott observed that 'We feel persuaded that if the points of the rocks and the rolling stones of the bathing place on the beach of this very delightful little watering place were removed, Clevedon would very soon double its number of visitors. There is also near the Rock House all the elements for the foundations of a pier and a landing place – much wanted.'

A pier had already been considered for the town in 1829 when Rutter had referred to a design by Wallis and Miles 'having been approved and adopted with a view to its immediate execution'. This did not materialise, however and the original Act for constructing the pier was not obtained until the parliamentary session of 1863–64.

In a now uncertain economy, business competition was fierce. Not only was a pier necessary as a tourist attraction but it was now proposed as a direct rail link between London and South Wales. The newly established local newspaper, *The Clevedon Mercury and Courier*, reported in November 1866 that a meeting was held at the Public Hall to discuss such a pier with an attendance 'of an influential and numerous character' . . . and . . . that it 'comprised a number of our capitalists and the whole of the principal tradesmen of the town. The chair was ably filled by Mr Charles Lempriere (chairman of the Aberystwyth and Tynmouth Pier Companies). He said an offer had been made to him of a pier which had been constructed for a foreign Government and thrown back on the hands of the contractors. It was 800 feet in length in 40 bays of 20 feet each. He was satisfied that the pier was such a one as would be of great service to them, and would certainly be a great saving of cost, the price being £6,000.'

This offer was eventually rejected on the grounds that it was too narrow and that its adaptation would be too expensive. The length of the pier had by then been marked out by the 'well known resident mariner' James Bullock with a marker buoy. The depth of water at 800 feet out at high water was, as Mr Bullock reported, 60 feet and *The Mercury* recorded that: 'The report of Mr James Bullock, who has placed a buoy out at 800 ft to show the public the distance, appears most satisfactory'. By February 1867 the preliminary work was well under way.

The Mercury reported that 'arrangements having now been made locally to vest this undertaking in gentlemen locally connected with and interested in Clevedon, estimates have been obtained for the construction of a strong and handsome pier, 840 feet in length at a cost covering all expenditure of about £10,000. The following gentlemen have consented to form a board of directors, viz: Sir A H Elton, Bart., Richard Godwin Esq., Samuel Ransford Esq., Mr John Maynard.' Such was the enthusiasm that three weeks later the newspaper was able to report that some £5,000 had been raised even though no prospectus had as yet been issued and by July 20th that several of the engineers and foremen had arrived on site . . . 'We hear that the Pier will be commenced on Monday'.

Clevedon Pier Company had appointed two enthusiastic London engineers, John William Grover and Richard Ward, to design the pier. Hamilton's Windsor Iron Works of Liverpool were selected to undertake the construction and erection of the ironwork and Ambrose Oliver of Hitcham, the stone abutments. Some twenty framed piers had by now been built, many by the master pier builder, Eugenius Birch, who had incorporated the first screw piles at Margate in 1853, and the engineers were fortunate in being able to use the lessons which had already been learnt. Lightness and a minimum resistance to wind and sea pressure had been shown to be all important in designing a strong structure which would withstand heavy gales. This was to be particularly important at Clevedon with a tidal range of up to 49 feet, one of the highest in the world and a current velocity of up to $5\frac{1}{2}$ m.p.h.

2/4 A very detailed record of the design exists in the paper presented by Grover at the Institute of Civil Engineers in 1871 together with drawings prepared at that time.[4] His design was based on the use of Barlow rails, a patent wrought iron rail section used by Brunel for parts of the wide gauge railways in South Wales and the West Country. Their hollow section apparently had a tendency to spread under load and perhaps for this reason they were replaced when the Great Western Railway switched to narrow gauge tracks. Why Grover decided to use the rails is uncertain but it is true that the choice of rolled wrought iron structural sections was limited at the time which is one reason why cast iron flanged columns were very common in piers.[5] Grover increased their strength by rivetting them back to back to form piles and by curving

4. See Appendix 2 for reprint of the ICE paper.

5. Wrought iron was only made in small batch quantities and it was difficult to obtain pieces large enough to roll into large sections. Steel production using the Bessemer Converter did not start until 1856 and had not, as yet, superseded wrought iron.

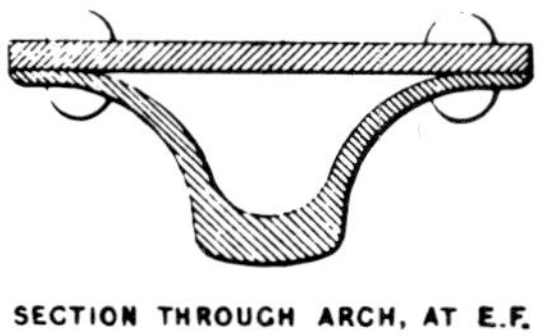

SECTION THROUGH ARCH, AT E.F.

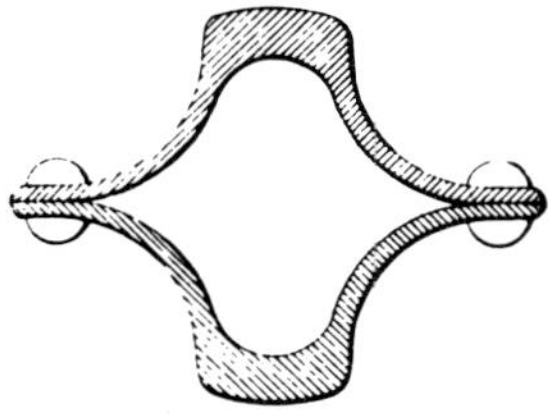

SECTION THROUGH PILE, AT A.B.

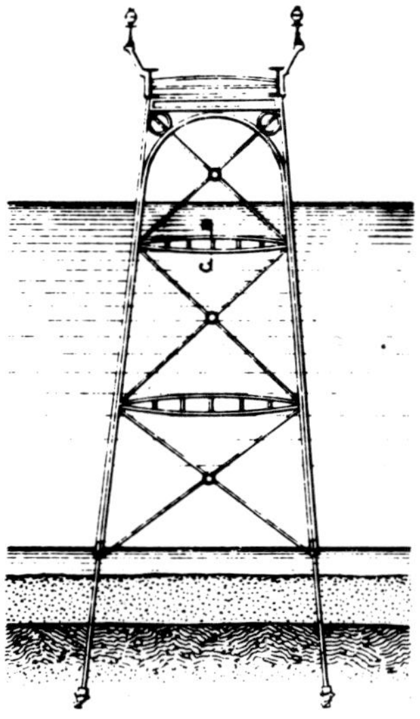

them and then rivetting them to curved iron flats to form the arched sections.
Trestles were built up in this way using a framework of four legs and were fixed 38–41
at 100 foot centres to form eight arches. The superstructure, resting on these trestles,
consisted of decking supported between the bottom flanges of two 3 ft 6 in deep
composite girders running the full length of the pier with the top flanges extended to
form continuous seats and balustrades.

The pier was built on magnesian limestone and below water the design was more
conventional. Each leg was fixed by a 5 in diameter wrought iron stem which was 45
attached to a 2 ft diameter cast iron screw pile. The attachment had to be very firm for
the piles were screwed in through the foreshore, down to bedrock, by turning the rod
until a $4\frac{1}{2}$ in rope, passing round 6 ft capstan bars, parted with the strain. The average
depth of the piles was 12 ft although the longest pile went down to a depth of 76 ft.
The original pier head was supported by 18 such wrought iron piles.

Each trestle had to be floated out into position and the girders floated out and
lifted by derrick and crane. The weather was critical and it took anything from the ten
days for number five span to three months per span when the weather was unfavourable.
Construction was nevertheless quite rapid and the works – a total of some 350 tons of
wrought iron – took only 18 months to complete with an average workforce of 60 men, 3
then a comparatively small number for a project of this size.

The Mercury recorded construction of the pier with due care and some impatience. Only three weeks after Hamilton's had started on site they complained . . . 'Agreeable with everything that takes place in Clevedon in the way of improvements, the Pier appears to make its way but slowly, notwithstanding the almost hourly visits of some one or other of the Directors and three assistant engineers. Some half dozen men in addition to foremen are the only hands on the job.' Progress was in fact slow during the first few months although by October 1867 the abutment had been completed. The work proceeded more rapidly towards the end of the year under resident engineer J Wallace Peggs and the supervision of Mr Twigg, who had been engaged in a variety of pier work and by November *The Mercury* was reporting again . . . 'Great progress is being made with the Clevedon Pier. Numerous are the obstacles that lie in the way – tides have to be depended upon, and every particle of iron has to be conveyed by manual labour to its destination. About 80 tons of the 500 to be used in the construction of the work has arrived, and the Beach, Esplanade and hill towards Wellington

Terrace present quite a remarkable appearance, being lined with vast quantities of wrought iron.'

Two weeks later it was reported that one side of a 100 ft span had been erected, and by August 1868 – only 12 months after the work had first started on site – 600 feet were completed.

This was not without considerable difficulties. Anthony Sheridan, one of the rivetters, is recorded as having saved three men from drowning. In *The Mercury* of March 21st 1868 the first fatal accident was described in some detail . . . 'Shocking Accident . . . Yesterday afternoon, about half past four, a labourer, named Henry Groves, met his death in a frightful manner. In the construction of these works an iron boat is used to convey the men to and from a barge and portions of the work at high water. This boat has from the first been an unfortunate expense by getting adrift, etc., it was therefore thought advisable to hoist it under the pier – and yesterday afternoon, at the time mentioned, a gang of men were engaged in this duty. A windlass, or crab, was used in the work and the deceased had hold of a portion of the rope known as the "slack". By some means the machinery of the crab slipped, and the drum pushed in an opposite direction, drawing the poor fellow round its narrow circumference, completely crushing him to death. The scene of the accident presents a sickening sight – the windlass is partially covered with blood, the planks of 200 ft being likewise sprinkled. A gloom has been cast over the entire works in consequence of this melancholy occurrence.'

With Clevedon exposed to the South West prevailing winds blowing off the Channel, gales presented a further problem. Grover was concerned that 'these circumstances, added to the bad holding nature of the ground, caused much delay; the stages being frequently destroyed and the boats and barge moored outside being driven ashore and wrecked'. The storm of August 1868 passed without damage to the pier itself, however, 'not the slightest vibration was to be felt in the whole 600 feet of the pier . . .'. By January 1869 the newspaper was reporting that 'the steps at the pier-head which were washed away during the late gales are now replaced. The entrance gates and turnstiles are also fixed and we hope to hear soon some tidings of its being opened'.

The workmen who suffered these hazards found themselves well looked after by the local community. Owen Roberts, the Clerk of the Works, installed a library at the baths. In June and December 1868 seventy rivetters, riggers and fliers sat down to a dinner provided by Mrs Perry, proprietress of the Old Rock House since her husband's death in 1864, and in response to her kindness the men presented her with a bible.

The construction of the abutments to the pier was not as hazardous as the pier itself but the design had changed from the simple stone abutment originally envisaged and now incorporated a toll-house with accommodation for the pier master. Built by
W Green of Clevedon, the builder who was also responsible for the town's bandstand, 2
it was designed by architect Hans Price of Weston-super-Mare in a Scottish baronial style much favoured at that time for bridge abutments. The romanticism of its design, highly representative of the period, contrasted strongly with the functional engineering of the pier. *The Mercury* aptly described it as having 'the look of stability in its favour' but considered that it 'reminds one painfully of a sham castle, very like those chalk
ornaments affixed to cakes'. 21/38

Despite this criticism Hans Price appears to have been active in Clevedon in the late 1860s. He is recorded as having been the architect of both the Market Hall, which
was opened two days after the pier, and Mrs Perry's new Rock House Hotel which 65
was to be opened shortly after in anticipation of the increased trade from the pier. 9
Price adopted a wide variety of architectural styles in these buildings and in his later work in Weston-super-Mare.[7]

The final components were the entrance gates and railings made in the Clevedon Foundry of Turner and Sons and at a meeting of the directors in February 1869 the contractors were able to hand over the Pier. *The Mercury* agitated once more, this time for a grand opening . . . 'form a committee . . . provide a banquet, a public procession and those other things that make a holiday famous'.

Only in early March was a committee formed to arrange the opening and time was short. On Easter Sunday snow fell but Mr Goodman, the pier master, was not alarmed and predicted fine weather. On Easter Monday, March 29th, the sun shone on all Clevedon. A general holiday had been declared and the town was festooned with flags and
decorations. Hundreds of carts poured in from the surrounding villages and towns. *The* 5
Mercury was able to record that 'the demonstration of yesterday consisted of a general holiday, a closing of houses of businesses and thorough decoration of the town; the following public bodies and gentry, also school children, walked in procession from the Railway Station, starting at 12.15: Police – 12 in number, Inhabitants and Visitors,

7. Hans Fowler Price 1835–1912 practised in Weston-super-Mare from 1862 and played a large part in the town's development. Two buildings which emphasise the variety of styles adopted by his later partnership were the Constitutional Club (originally Masonic Hall) of 1881 designed in what might be called a Bavarian style, and the Mercury Offices of 1885, a hundred yards away in Weston's Boulevard, designed in a Moorish style perhaps reflecting the partners' more recent travels.

Clevedon Artillery and Band – 54, Bristol Artillery Band, Nailsea Engineers and Band – 94, Odd Fellows – 90, Pier Directors, Weston Pier Directors, Axbridge Drum and Fife Band, Committee of Demonstration – 28, Children of various schools – 500.'

The procession wound its way past decorated shops and through triumphal arches of evergeen. On reaching the pier the opening ceremony was performed by the directors and at 3 o'clock there followed a dinner for one hundred guests, including both William Grover and Hans Price, in the Rock Hotel. Several hundred more of the participants sat down to a 'capital cold collation' provided by John Maynard, one of the directors, in the new Market Hall and the local school children were assembled in tents in Herbert Gardens and each given 'a 3d piece and a bun.'

During the day several thousand people visited the town but 'everything passed off exceedingly well' and in the evening the celebrations continued with illuminations and fireworks, the pier being brilliantly lit by eight arches of gas jets and the entrance by an illuminated sign which read 'Success to the Pier'. *The Mercury* was delighted. 'Thus ended the greatest gala day Clevedon has ever experienced, and we say, in the words of one of the speakers at the Pier Dinner, we believe it is the commencement of better times for our fair Clevedon'.

The pier was relatively successful and in 1872 it received 40,000 visitors. The author of the 1880 *Clevedon Guide* went to great lengths to publicise the particular attractions of the pier: 'Many places of interest are accessible by water from the Clevedon Pier, among which we may mention Chepstow, with its castle and Tintern Abbey 20 miles distant; Newport with its docks, 9 miles; Cardiff, with its castle, docks and shipping, 16 miles; Weston-super-Mare, 6 miles; the Steep and Flat Holmes, with its light-house and batteries, 12 miles; Lynton and Lynmouth, with the Valley of Rocks, 44 miles; Ilfracombe with its tors, 50 miles; Swansea, with its docks and copper works, 58 miles; Tenby with its sands and scenery and adjacent Caldy Island, 90 miles.'

Its financial success was short lived however and by 1890 the shareholders of Clevedon Pier Company were anxious to pass on their burden to the Local Government Board. Wild claims were made that the pier was unsafe. Certainly the wrought iron which has been so suitable for the pier had not proved as successful for the head which now needed strengthening. A meeting of ratepayers was called to discuss the fate of 'their poor old pier' – a scene which was to be repeated nearly one hundred years later –

and Mr Eustace Button moved 'That this meeting requests and authorises the Local Board to apply for a Town's Act for Clevedon, to enable them to treat for the purchase of the Pier.' The motion was carried almost unanimously.

In March 1891 a specially convened meeting of the Local Board was held to consider the proposition that the offer of the Pier Company to dispose of their undertaking for £700 be accepted. Sir Edmund Elton, the largest shareholder, however, purchased the remaining shares and made a present of the pier to the town. Tenders were invited by the Local Board to renew the pier head in cast iron, this time at an angle with the pier in line with the current, and replace the decking. Mr Double of Ipswich secured the contract and completed it 12 months later. The re-opening in April 1893 was **10–13**
carried out with almost as much ceremony as the original opening.

At this time there were still no pier head buildings and it was not until the summer of 1894 that these were completed. *The Mercury* had remarked earlier in that year that the new pavilion and shelter seats promised to be of a 'pretty appearance' . . . adding considerably to the attractiveness of this, the best pier in the Bristol Channel. These new additions by contractors McDowell and Stevens of the Melton Iron Works, built under the supervision of the Town Surveyor, were mainly in ornamental iron work and weighed some 26 tons. Their design, with roofs which were predominantly **15**
Japanese in appearance, was a mixture of several styles carrying on the tradition started some hundred years earlier with John Nash's Brighton Pavilion.

The pier was now complete, the crenellated castle and heavy abutments at one end, the Japanese pavilion at the other and the light, elegant wrought iron pier in between. It was not immune from the ravages of the gales, however, and the storm in January 1899 ripped up 20 feet of decking near the toll house. The new timber landing stage deteriorated rapidly and was wrecked by a further gale in 1910. Temporary repairs were carried out to maintain the steamer traffic and eventually a contract was entered into with Hobrough and Co. of Gloucester for the construction of a landing stage in the relatively new material of ferro-concrete using the Hennebique systems.

The contractors suffered problems with winds and rough seas, as Grover had done some 40 years earlier, but had the additional problem of mixing the concrete on the pier head. When the work was practically completed a gale blew up wrecking the still wet concrete and ripping up decking. Much of the work had to be dismantled and

22–23 a new start made but, by April 30th 1913, the pier was officially re-opened yet again
28 and the steamer *Waverley* was the first to arrive with due ceremony.

The steamers operating from the pier continued to be popular for many years until the collapse of the two last spans under test in 1970. Mr S C Smith-Cox, the Chairman and Managing Director of P & A Campbell Ltd. who for many years ran the steamers in the channel, records Saturday August 16th 1930 as a typical day in the life of the pier. 'At 10.45 a steamer went to Weston, Barry, Lynmouth and Ilfracombe' . . . at the same time, virtually . . . 'another steamer was scheduled to leave for Bristol. At 1.15 yet another visit was made to Cardiff, Penarth, Lynmouth and Ilfracombe and at 2.05 a further steamer proceeded to Weston and Barry Pier. During the evening a steamer left Clevedon for Weston at 6.30, also for an evening cruise, calling at Cardiff. At 8.35 there was an evening cruise to Bristol, at 8.50 a single trip to Portishead and Bristol; at 10.20 a further single trip to Bristol and at 10.35 a single trip to Penarth and Cardiff.'

24–29 The steamers and the pier played an important part in the life of the town at that time. A local resident Mr George Bees, recalls that several hundred people would arrive on the evening trip from Cardiff. Some would take cabs to local inns such as the Star at Tickenham but a late return meant missing the ferry and a long rail journey back home. Nevertheless many cross channel romances flourished. A dance hall with a penny organ on the pier head was extremely popular around this time, the spray splashing between the decking at high tide being an extra attraction. Many local people learnt to dance in the hall but when a proper floor was added attendance dwindled rapidly.

In financial terms, the pier was never the success that was anticipated although for many years it did pay for itself. In 1953–54 expenditure was £1,542 with an income of £1,513 but the gap widened despite a record number of 81,000 visitors in 1959–60. By 1967–68 the loss was claimed to be over £3,000 on an income of £1,600 but it appears that maintenance work accounted by the local authority to the pier included maintenance of many of the other sea front amenities as well. Actual maintenance on the pier does in any event appear to have been inadequate.

In the 1950s the consulting engineers to Clevedon UDC instituted a programme of testing in order to obtain insurance cover. Every other year temporary water tanks were erected to simulate the agreed load. Should any movement occur the load could be released. On October 17th 1970 the pier was again tested and polythene tubing filled with water used to produce the required load at 50 lb per square foot. The seventh trestle started to move and the water moved correspondingly. This increased the pressure until the trestle eventually collapsed taking two complete spans, 200 feet of the pier, down to the sea bed. 60

The pier was immediately closed down. This event produced considerable local response and fund raising was started almost immediately. By 1975 the Clevedon Pier Preservation Trust, formed in 1972, had managed to raise over £70,000 but the cost of repair was racing ahead with inflation. Following the hand-over of the pier to Woodspring District Council, after local government reorganisation in 1974, a survey was carried out by their engineer and cost estimates prepared. An estimate prepared in 1979 was in the region of £750,000, a figure no doubt increased by the failure to carry out any significant maintenance since the collapse.

The current status of the pier as a Grade II* listed building raised hopes of a considerable grant from central government but this did not materialise and in 1979 Woodspring District Council, ironically the very authority whose statutory duty it is to enforce the maintenance of listed buildings, applied to the Secretary of State for permission to demolish. The result was a Public Inquiry in March 1980 at which the Clevedon Pier Technical Group, supported and financed by the Preservation Trust, presented outline technical proposals for the restoration of the pier. The case for saving the pier was overwhelming and the Inspector stated in his findings that this 'exceptionally important building' with its 'unique' and 'delicate design' should be saved from demolition. 'The Clevedon Pier Preservation Trust would then have the opportunity of putting in hand their conserving operation and the Clevedon Pier Technical Group would then have time to work out and implement their proposals for restoration in detail'.

At the time of writing, the Trust and Technical Group are negotiating with Woodspring District Council in order to obtain a lease of the pier and commence the now desperately needed restoration work on a rolling programme. 61

Once again as in 1867 the future of the pier relies on the support and efforts which local people can themselves mobilise but nationally Clevedon Pier is gradually being appreciated both in terms of its relevance as a piece of nineteenth-century engineering and as a fine example of the pier building era. This will certainly help its chances of survival. Simon Adamson, in his report on the remaining seaside piers to the Victorian

Society, calls it 'undoubtedly the most graceful pier in the country' and this is an opinion which is shared by many leading authorities[6]. Sir John Betjeman puts Clevedon with Brighton's West Pier as the 'two most beautiful pleasure piers on the coast of England', the CBA Advisory Panel on Industrial Monuments places it with Bangor and Brighton West as one of the three piers in the country 'worthy of Grade I listing'* (see appendix 3).

6. See Appendix 3 for further quotations.

Clevedon Pier, in addition to its significance in any survey of the remaining seaside piers, is also locally important because of its links with Brunel but even more important is the role of the pier in maintaining the Victorian character of Clevedon.

The decline of Clevedon as a resort in the early twentieth century, when people from Bristol and Bath started to travel further afield. has meant that both pier and town have remained relatively unaltered. Clevedon is still essentially a small Victorian resort in character and its pier still reflects this domestic scale and parklike setting. In more publicised resorts such characteristics have been obscured by a veneer of twentieth century commercialism and extensive rebuilding. Clevedon and its pier remain as examples of the restrained simplicity which must have existed at other small resorts of the nineteenth century and continue to illustrate a relatively unconsidered aspect of Victorian life. ●

1. View of Clevedon from behind the Parish Church shortly after the pier was built in 1869 showing the open wooded nature of the upper town centre and the relationship of the housing and pier to the hill. ▶

1867 ~ 1893

2. Grover's proposed pier as it appeared in 'Engineering' December 1867: note the early scheme for the masonry approach which was later amended to include the toll house.

3. Workmen involved in the construction of the pier: lent by local builder Mr W Tinkling whose grandfather, a fisherman named Alfred Feltham, was employed in the construction as a labourer and is just discernible in the centre of this faded print.

4. Grover's design as presented to the Institute of Civil Engineers in March 1871: the design was based on the use of 'Barlow Rails' a patent wrought iron railway line introduced by W H Barlow in the early days of railways and used by Brunel on the Great Western. Details A, B and E, F show how they were adapted.

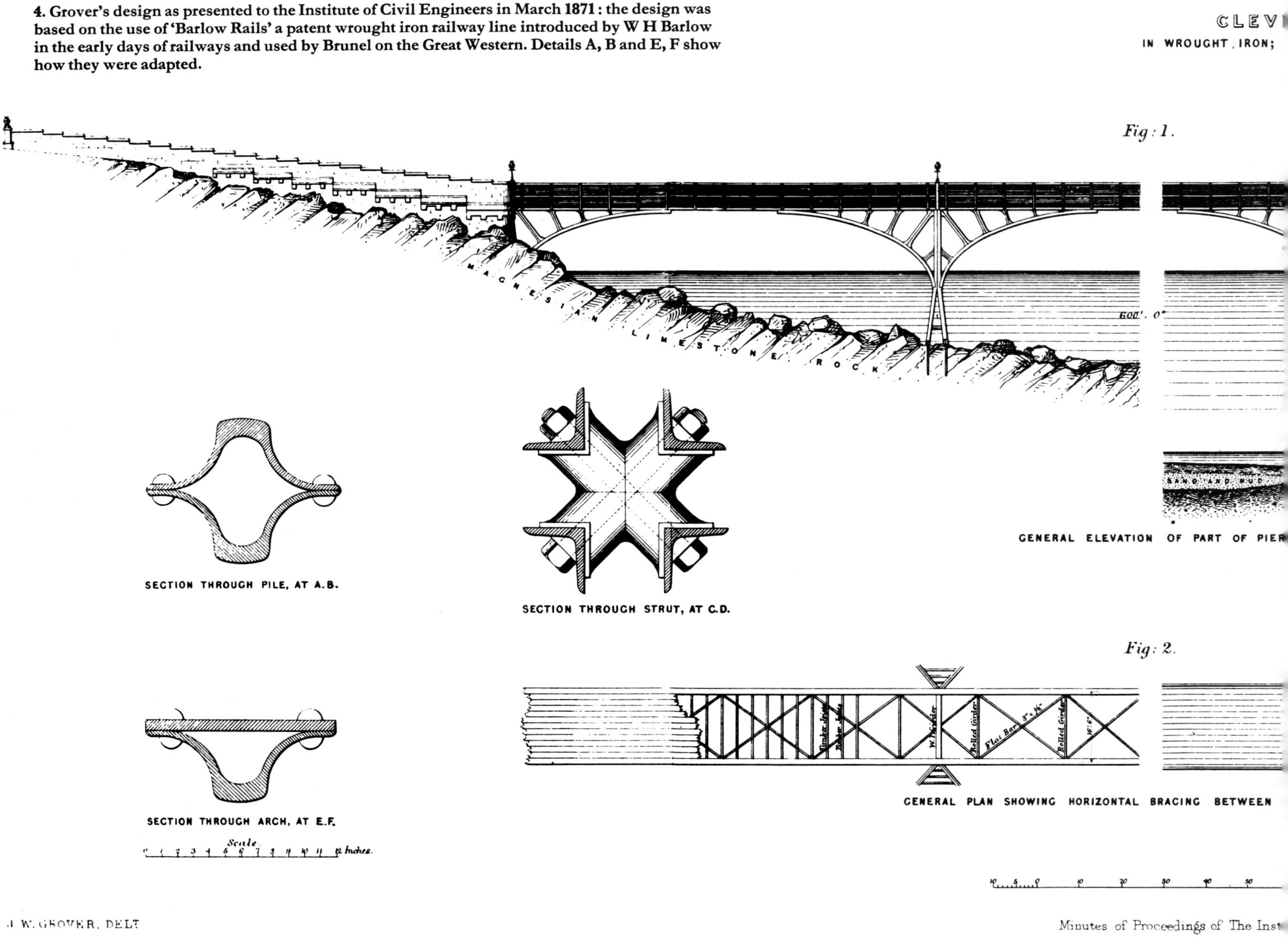

N PIER.

SPANS OF 100 FEET EACH.

PLATE 10.

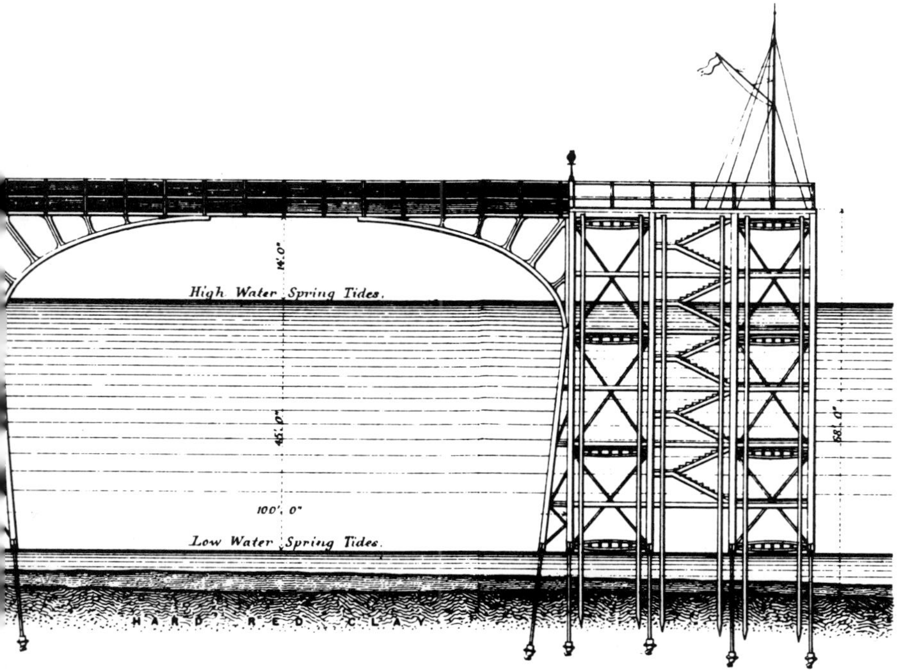

Fig: 3.

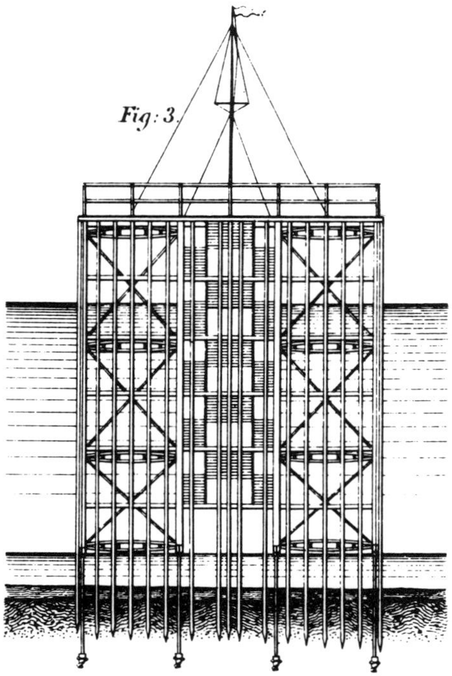

FRONT ELEVATION OF HEAD.

Fig: 4.

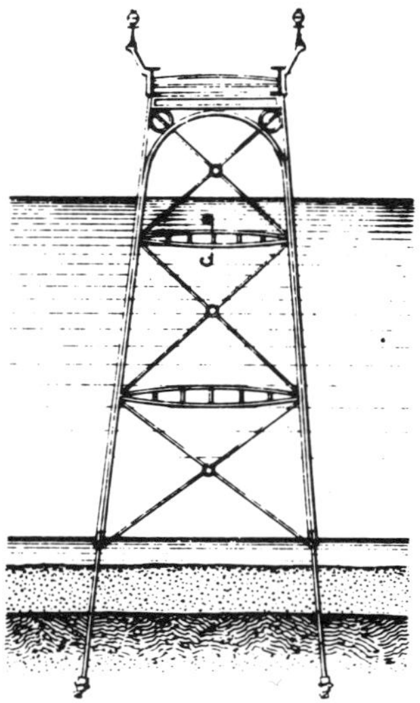

CROSS SECTION.

DERS.

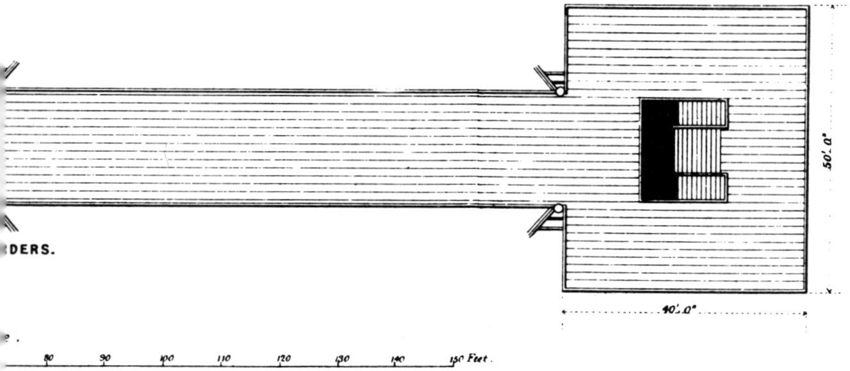

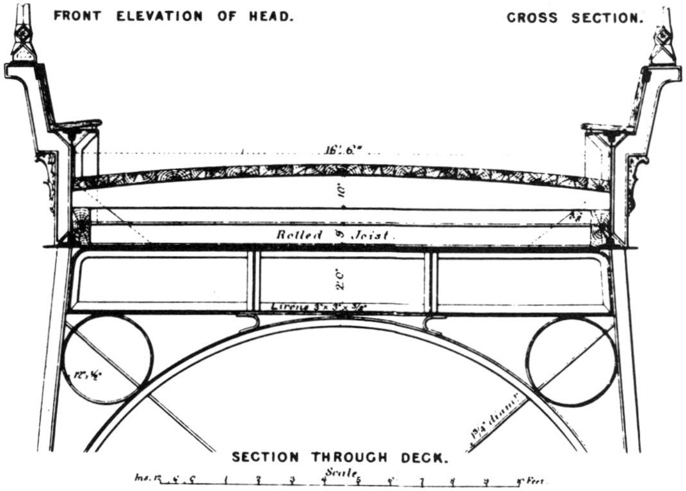

SECTION THROUGH DECK.

KELL BROS LITHRS CASTLE ST HOLBORN

5. Opening of the pier on Easter Monday March 29th 1869 as featured in the London Illustrated News.

A Chinaman travelled to Clevedon Pier,
And offered to work for a shilling a year;
So they gave him employ,
All the year as a buoy,
Bobbing and floating near Clevedon Pier.

6. Clevedon Pier as illustrated in 'Nonsense near Home' by Sir Arthur Hallam Elton in 1872.

7. The pier in 1890: the original pier head was soon to be replaced by a more substantial cast iron one with pavilion and shelters.

8.

9.

8. Postcard of around early **1893**: the new cast iron head had just been completed although the pavilions have not yet been started.

9. The Old Rock House Inn was replaced by the Royal Pier Hotel in **1869** to meet the anticipated increase in trade brought about by the pier.

1893 ~ 1967

10.

10. The re-opening of the pier by Lady Elton in April **1893** following construction of the cast iron pier head.

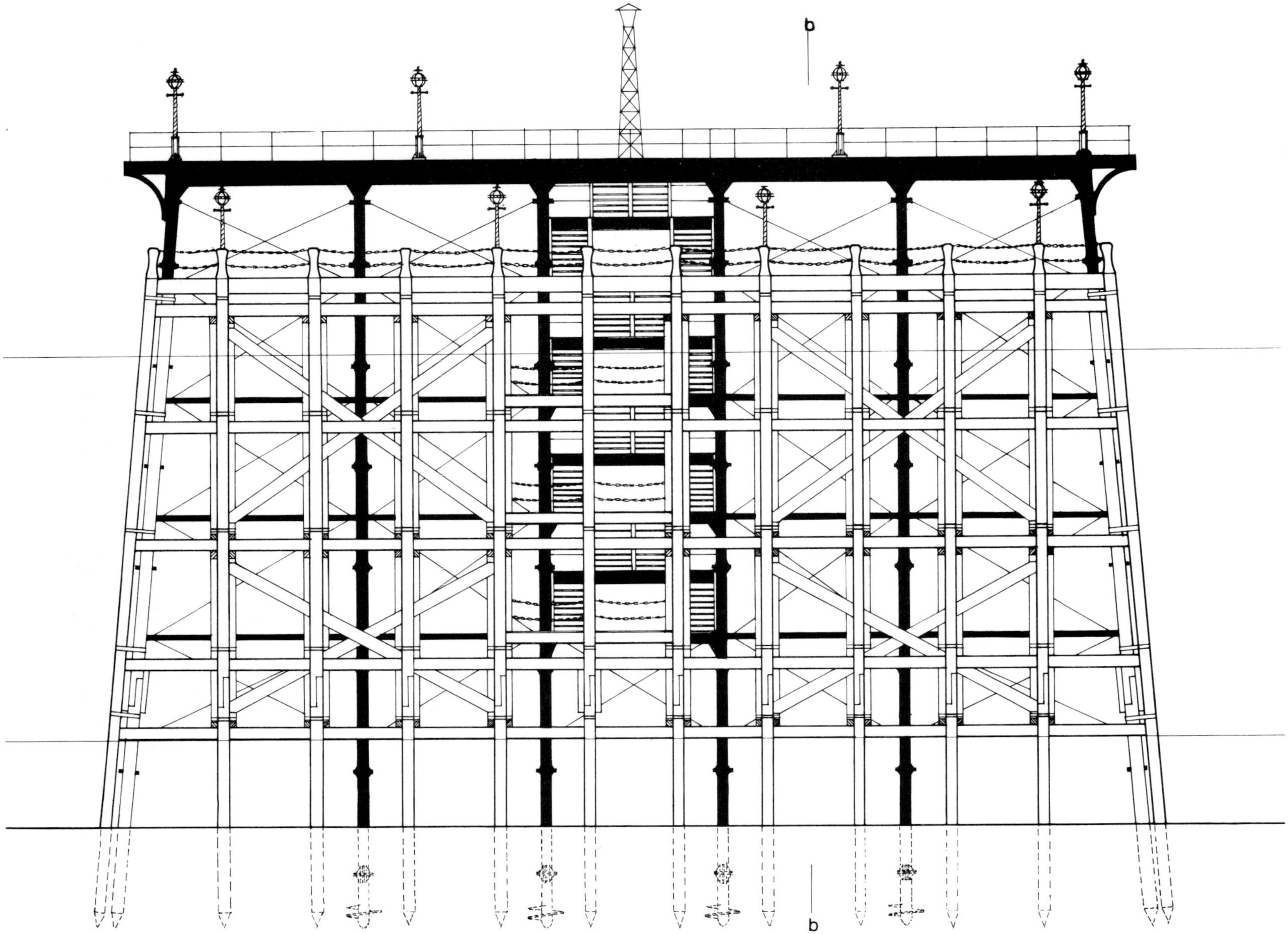
b
b

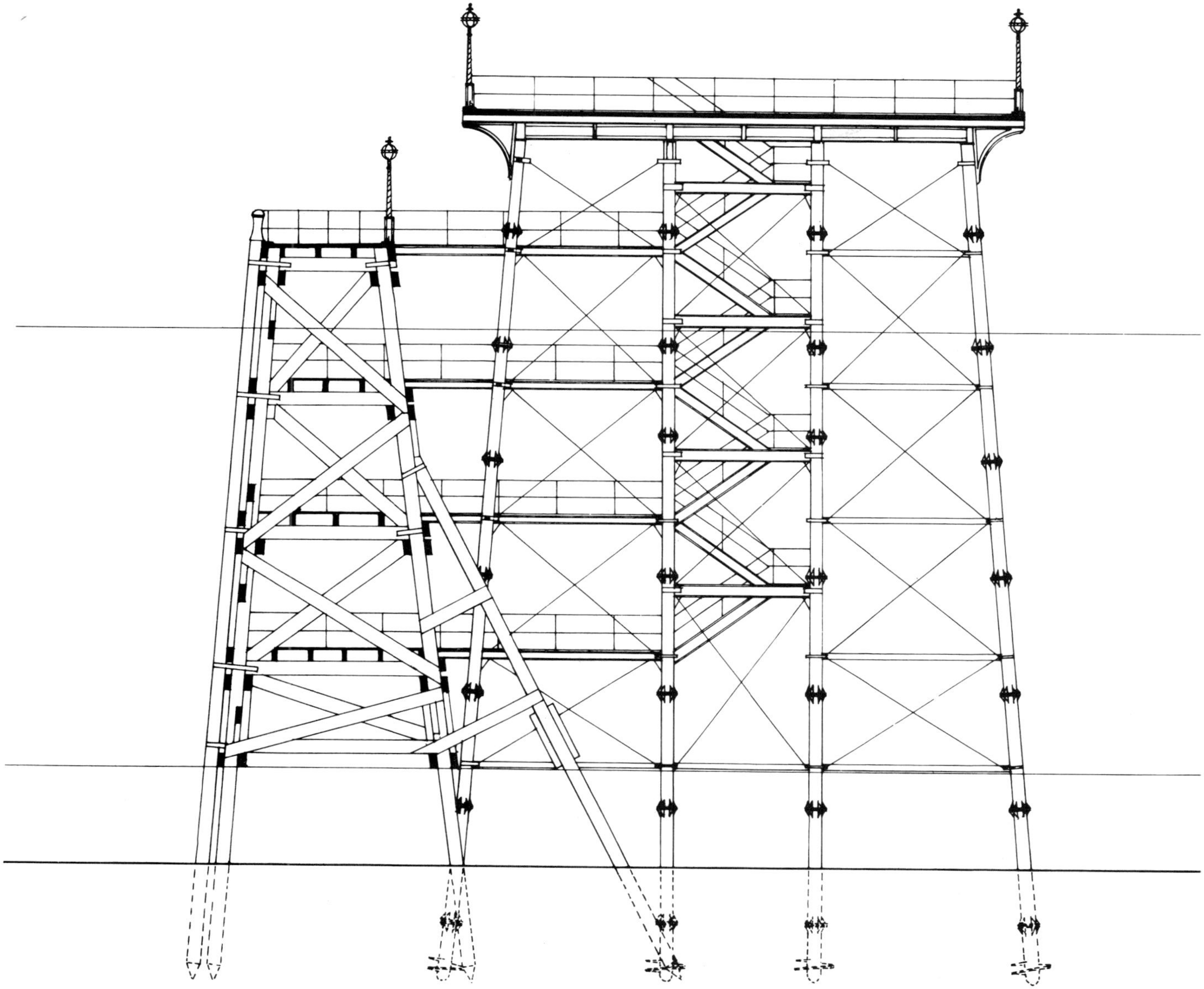

11/12. Design of the new cast iron pier head and timber landing stage as built in **1892–3**: illustrations based on the original working drawings. The pavilion and shelters were added shortly afterwards in **1894** and the timber landing stage was to be later replaced by a concrete one.

Pile at Pier head

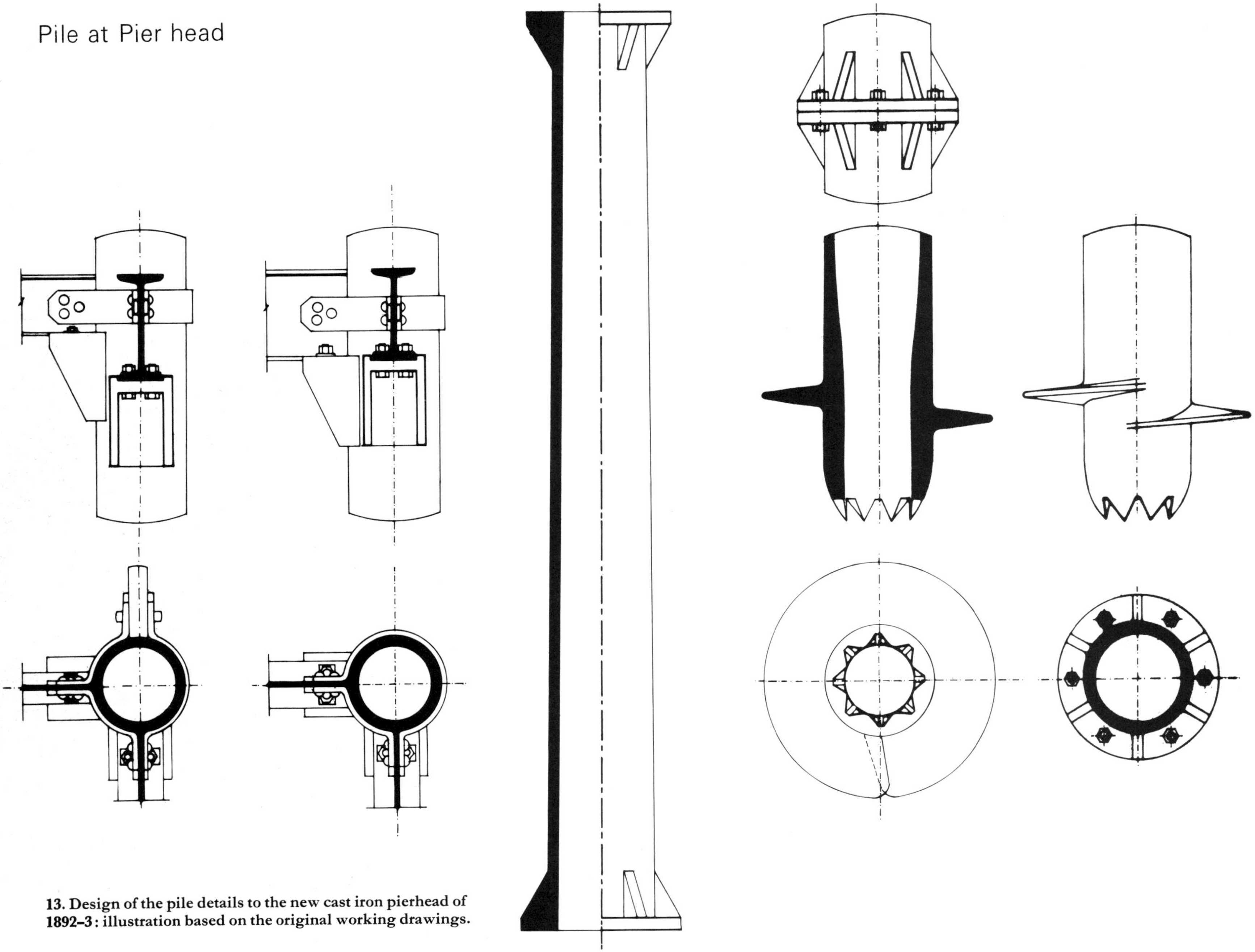

13. **Design of the pile details to the new cast iron pierhead of 1892–3: illustration based on the original working drawings.**

14. Engraving showing the cast iron pierhead together with the new pavilion and shelters of 1894.

15.

15. Design for the new cast iron pavilion as built by contractors McDowell & Stevens of the Melton Ironworks and completed in 1894: see the more recent detail photographs taken in 1967. The Mercury described it in 1894 as being 'of pretty appearance and adding considerably to the attractiveness of this, the best pier in the Bristol Channel'.

16.

17.

16. Postcard showing the pier complete with the new pierhead pavilion and shelters added in **1894**.

17. Postcard looking along the pier with the cast iron shelters in the foreground.

Clevedon looking N

18.

19.

Green Beach, Clevedon

CLEVEDON. Green Beach.

20.

21.

D_45755. C

18/19/20. Postcards from the **1905–12** period showing the atmosphere around the promenade adjacent to the pierhead.

22.

21. Postcard showing the pier entrance and Royal Pier Hotel: The dance hall had now been added on the pierhead.

23.

22/23. Opening of the reinforced concrete landing stage by Colonel William Long C.M.G. on April 30th **1913**: built at a cost of about £3,000. This replaced the timber landing stage damaged by gales in **1910**.

29.

Royal Pier Hotel,

CLEVEDON (ADJOINING THE PIER).

Most convenient for joining the Steamers from BRISTOL, which call Daily for ILFRACOMBE, LYNMOUTH, CARDIFF, TENBY, MINEHEAD, etc., etc.

Every Accommodation.

Moderate Terms.

En Pension.

N.B. A separate part of the Hotel reserved for Outing Parties. Terms on Application.

Apply, **MANAGER.**

26.

28. Steamer Waverley coming in to landing stage during the opening ceremony of **1913**.

24. Postcard from Cardiff dated **1907** referring to the steamer traffic.

25/26/27. Postcard of steamer leaving pier, photographs of boat arriving and pier deckhand.

29. Advertisement for the Royal Pier Hotel referring to convenience for steamer passengers **1903**.

24.

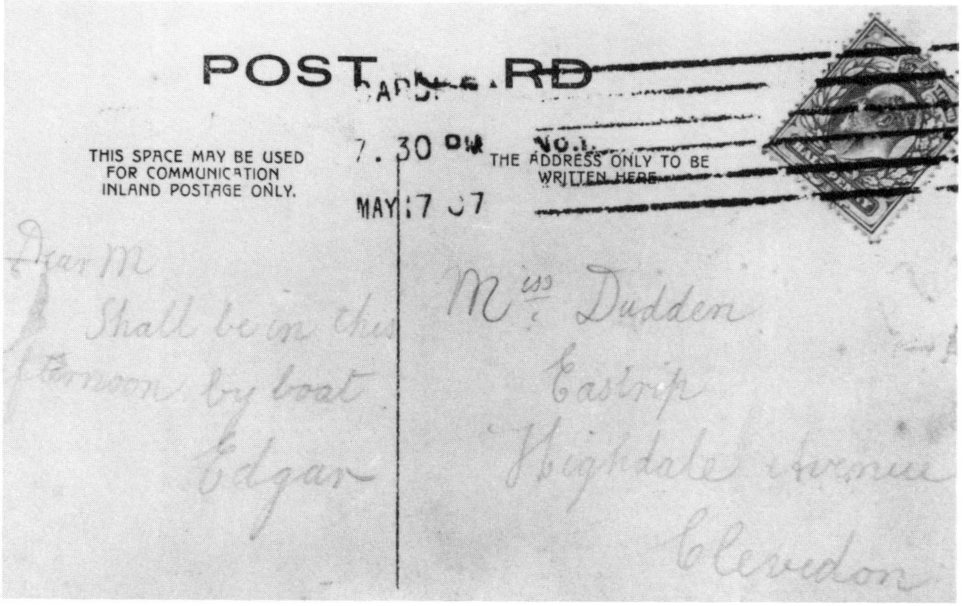

25.

30. Captain Boyton.

31. Aerial view of pier taken on its centenary in 1969.

1967–1970

32/33. The pier in 1967.

35.

34. Details of the cast iron legs to the pierhead and diagonal braces.

35. View looking under the pier towards the head showing the tapered cross members between the wrought iron legs. The cast iron trestle in the foreground was added to support the first span in **1948**.

36.

37.

36. View looking back towards the toll-house with the Royal Pier Hotel to the left. The fishermen were a regular sight on the pier, catching congers or strange varieties such as the butterfly gurnard with red and blue tinted wings. In **1969** the pier was being used by about one hundred anglers per week.

37. Side view looking towards the head with the support trestle added in **1948** to the right.

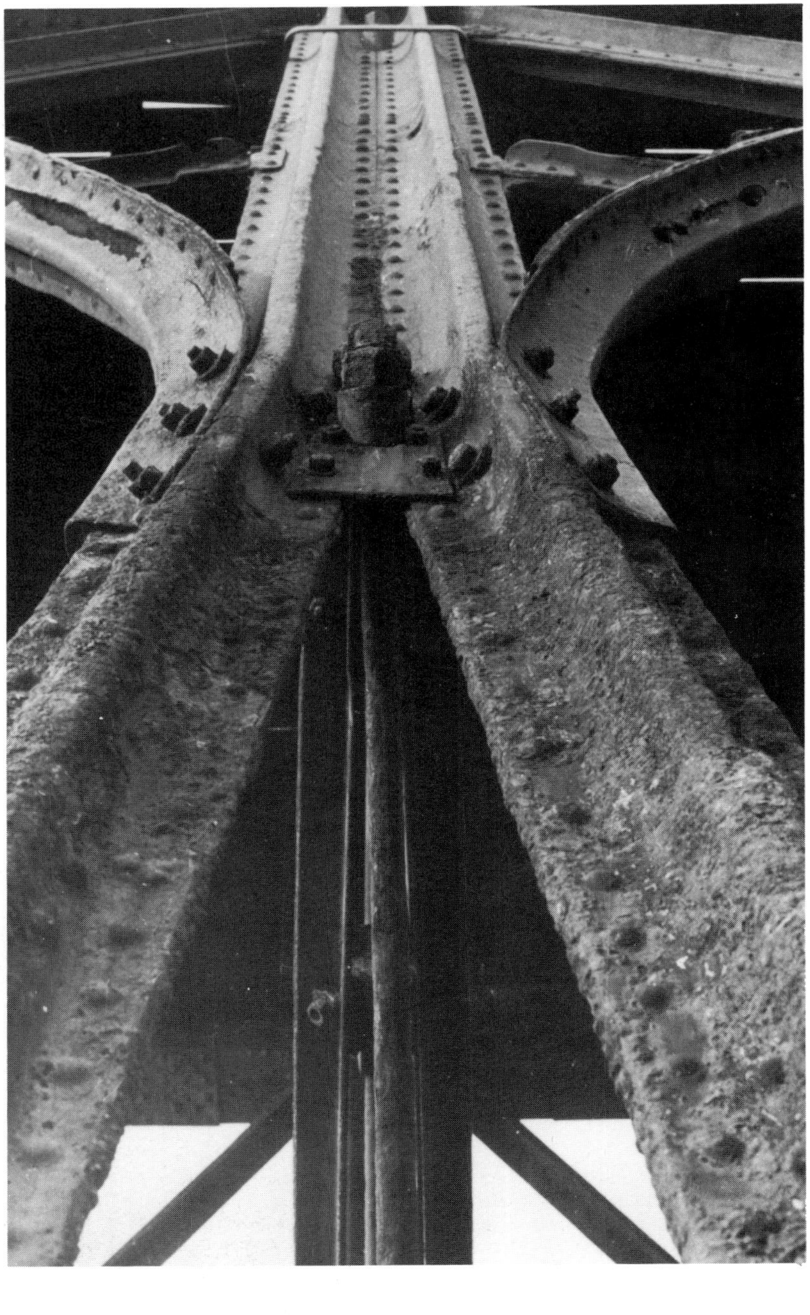

38/39.

40.

41.

38–41. Details of the trestles constructed from wrought iron 'Barlow Rails' and detail of tie bar connection — as photographed in 1967.

43.

44.

42. Section of the flights of steps in the pierhead linking through to the landing stage: these allowed a landing to be made at almost any stage of the tide despite the tidal range of up to **49** feet — one of the highest in the world.

43. Detail of column and tie to trestle in first bay of pier.

44. Detail of cast iron column to pierhead.

45/46.

47.

45. Pile connection at the base of a wrought iron trestle.

46. Strap detail.

47. The pierhead pavilion in 1967 with the continuous seating and balustrade in the foreground.

8. 49.

50.

48/49. Details of the pavilion's staircase and balusters.

50. One of the two cast iron pagoda style shelter seats in 1967.

51.

52.

53.

54. 55.

51/52. Details of the cast iron shelter seats.

53. Cast iron column and head to the first floor of the pavilion.

54. Side of cast iron lamp base on the pier recording the names of the engineers. Other panels record the name of the contractor.

55. Cast iron side panel to shelter seat.

57.

58.

56.

59.

56–59. Steamer embarkation, Summer 1967

60. Pier shortly following collapse of two spans during load test: October 1970.

1970-80

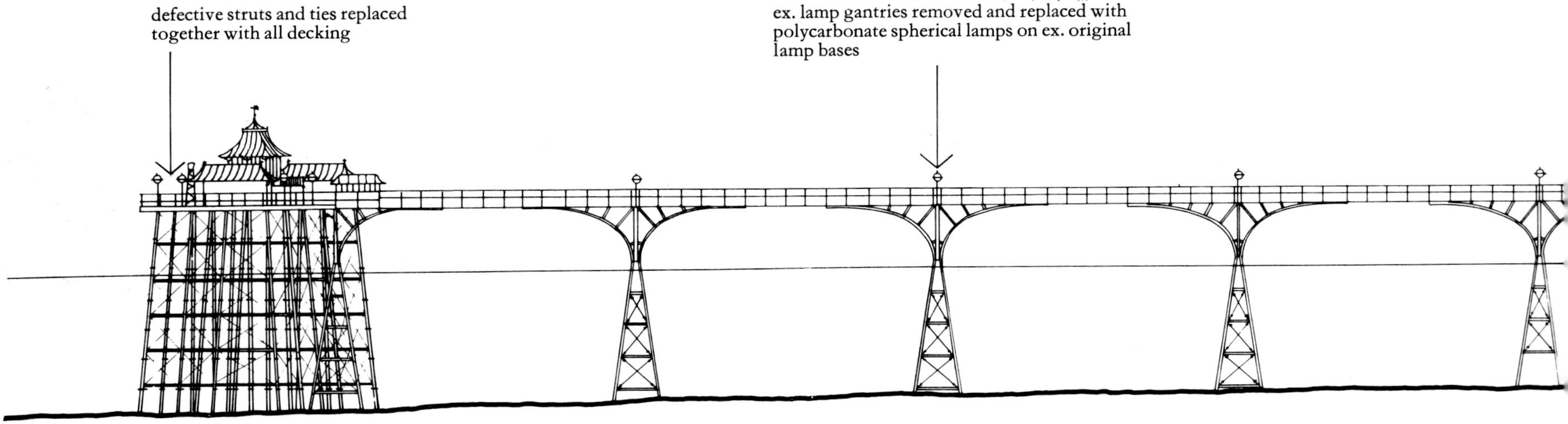

west elevation

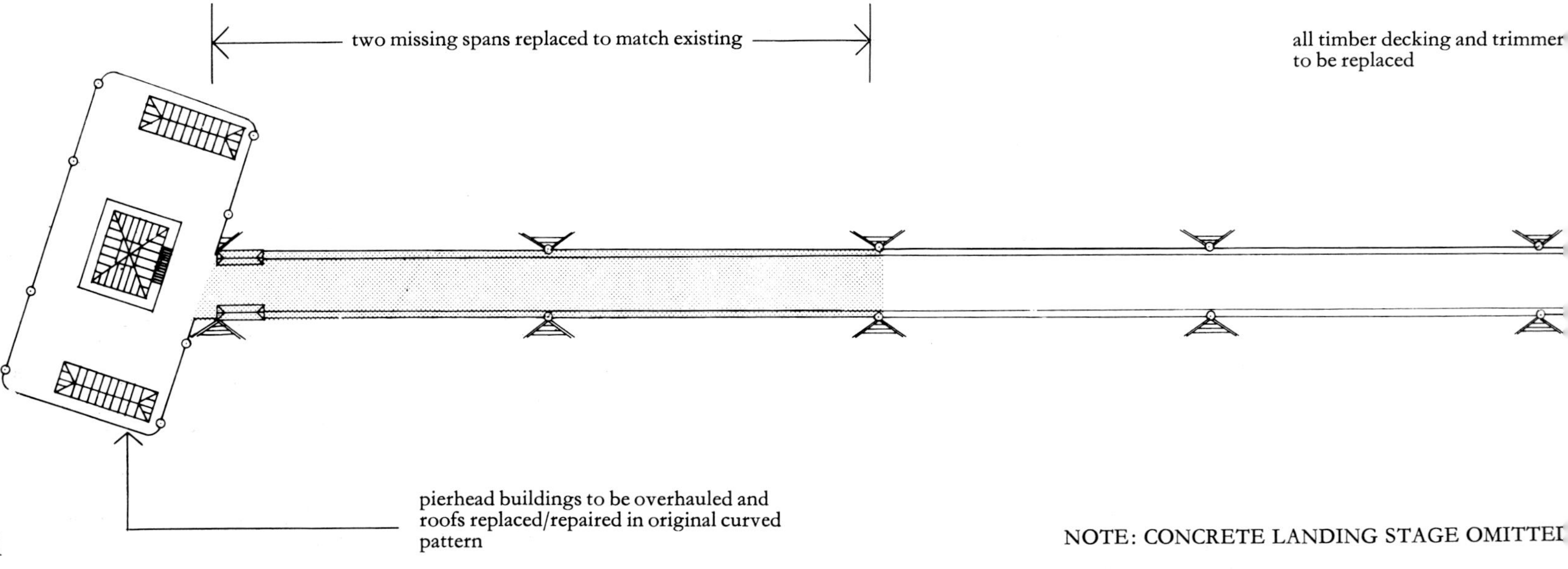

plan

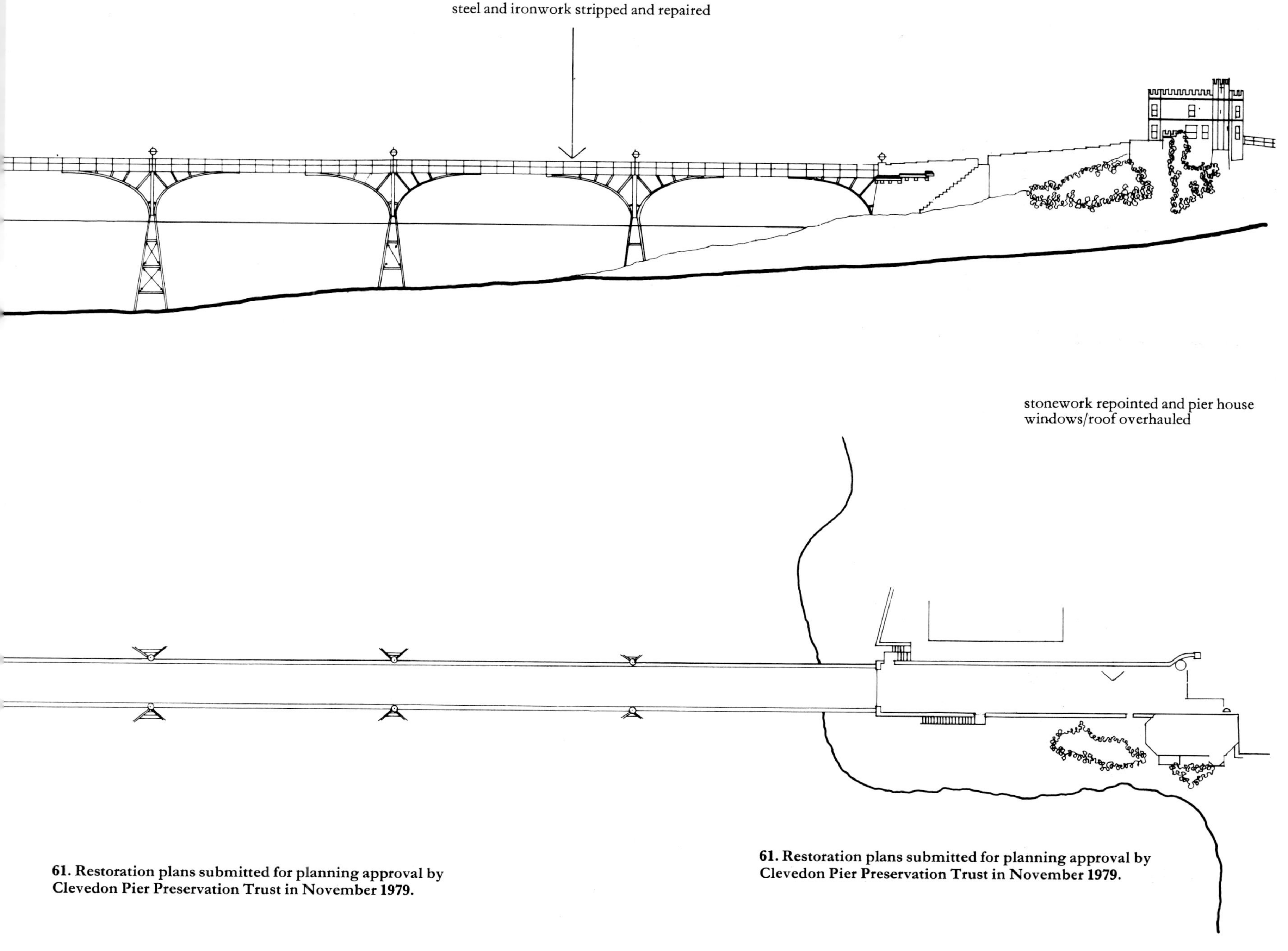

61. Restoration plans submitted for planning approval by Clevedon Pier Preservation Trust in November 1979.

61. Restoration plans submitted for planning approval by Clevedon Pier Preservation Trust in November 1979.

62.

65.

64.

63.

Victorian Clevedon as it remains today:

62–4. Examples of the variety and interest of timber bargeboards and eaves detail still remaining.

65. The Market Hall: it was used for the dinner which marked the pier opening and was itself officially opened two days later on March 31st 1869 with a display of fireworks on the pier head to the strains of the Clevedon Artillery Band. It was designed by the same architect responsible for the toll house, Hans Price, and plans are now being prepared by Woodspring District Council for its restoration.

66. A typical view of Victorian Clevedon: to the left is the church of St John the Evangelist, designed by William Butterfield and completed in 1878.

Appendix 1: Clevedon Pier in the chronological list of remaining piers

* *Piers demolished*

Pier	Original Length	Built	Engineer	Contractor
Ryde	1250	1813–14		
***Brighton Chain**	1134	1896	S Brown	MacIntosh/Brown
***Southend (1)**	1800	1887		
***Walton-on-Naze (1)**	330	1830		
***Herne Bay**	3613	1831–2	T Telford	
***Deal** (**1**)	250	1838	J Rennie	
Great Yarmouth Wellington	700	1853–4	P Ashcroft	
***Margate**		1853–6	E Birch	Bastow/direct
***Great Yarmouth Britannia (1)**	700	1857–8	A W Morant	G Allen
Southport	3600	1859–60	J Brunlees	W & J Galloway
***Bournemouth (1)**	1000	1859–61	G Rennie	D Thornbury
Worthing	960	1861–2	R Rawlinson	J Cliff
Blackpool North	1410	1862–3	E Birch	R Laidlaw
Brighton West	1115	1863–6	E Birch	R Laidlaw
***Deal** (**2**)	1100	1863–4	E Birch	R Laidlaw
***Ryde Victoria**	900	*c*1864		
Aberystwyth	800	1864–5	E Birch	J E Dowson
Bognor	1000	1864–5	J W Wilson	J E Dowson

* *Piers demolished*

Pier	Original Length	Built	Engineer	Contractor
***Lytham**	900	1864–5	E Birch	R Laidlaw
Teignmouth	600	1865–7	J W Wilson	
Eastbourne	1000	1866–72	E Birch	J E Dowson Head Wrightson
***Scarborough**	1000	1866–9	E Birch	J E Dowson Head Wrightson
***New Brighton**		1866–7	E Birch	J E Dowson
Blackpool Central	1518	1867–8	J I Mawson	R Laidlaw
CLEVEDON	842	1867–8	R J WARD J W GROVER	HAMILTON'S WINDSOR IRONWORKS
***Rhyl**	2355	1867	J Brunlees	R Laidlaw
Weston-super-Mare Birnbeck	1350 plus island	1867	E Birch	Isca Iron Co
Saltburn	1400	1868–7		
***Douglas**	1000	1869	J Dixon	J Dixon
Hastings	910	1869–72	E Birch	R Laidlaw
***Westward Ho'**	493	1870–3	J W Wilson	Gooch, J Abbott
Totland Bay		*c*1870	S H & S W Yockney	
***Hunstanton**	830	1870–1	J W Wilson	
Clacton		1871	P S Bruff	

* *Piers demolished*

Pier	Original Length	Built	Engineer	Contractor
Redcar	1300	1871–3	J E & A Dowson	Head Wrightson
Cleethorpes	1200	1872–5		
Ventnor		1872		
Morecambe Central	912	*c*1872		
***Coatham**	1800	1873–5		
Herne Bay (2)	320	1873	Wilkinson & Smith	Direct labour
***Withernsea**	1196	1875–8	T Cargill	J O Gardiner
***Aldeburgh**	561	1876–8	T Cargill	G W Hutchinson
Llandudno	2295	1876–8	Brunlees & McKerrow	J Dixon
Yarmouth	665	1876		J Denham
Bournemouth	838	1878–9	G S Bridgeman	J Harris
Sandown	360	1878		
Southsea South Parade	600	1878	G Rake	Head Wrightson
***Hornsea**		1879	E Birch	Bergheim
***Ramsgate**	550	1879–81	H Robinson	Head Wrightson
***Sea View**	1000	1880	F Caws	Various
Skegness	1802	1880–1	Clarke & Pickwell	Head Wrightson
Ramsey	2150	1882		Head Wrightson

** Piers demolished*

Pier	Original Length	Built	Engineer	Contractor
***Plymouth**	465	1884	E Birch	
***Lee-on-Solent**	750	1885–8	Galbraith & Church	J Robinson
St Annes-on-Sea		1885		
***Folkestone**	683	1887–8	M N Ridley G Chatterton	Heenan & Froude
***Southend (2)**	6600	1887–8	J Brunlees	Arrol Bros
Boscombe	600	1888–9	A Smith	E Howell
***St Leonards**	950	1888–91	R St G Moore	Head Wrightson
***Southbourne**	300	1888	A Smith	E Howell
Brighton Palace	1760	1891–1901	R St G Moore	A Mayoh
Shanklin	1200	1891		
Blackpool South	429	1892–3	T P Worthington	J Butler
***Dover**	900	1893	J J Webster	A Thorne
***Morecambe West End**	1800	1893–6	J Harker	Mayoh & Haley Widness Foundry Co
Swanage	642	1893		
Penarth	650	1894	H F Edwards	J & A Mayoh
Walton-on-Naze (2)	800	1895		J Cochrane

** Piers demolished*

Pier	Original Length	Built	Engineer	Contractor
Bangor	1500	1896	J J Webster	A Thorne
Herne Bay (3)	3787	1896–9	E Matheson	Head Wrightson
***Rhos-on-Sea**		1896	J Dixon	
Mumbles	835	1897–8	W S Marsh	Mayoh & Haley Widnes Foundry Co
***Bexhill**		1898	Mayoh & Haley	
Colwyn Bay	220	1899	Maynall & Littlewood	Widnes Foundry Co
Cromer	500	1900–1	Douglass & Arnott	A Thorne
Great Yarmouth Britannia (2)		1900–2	Mayoh & Haley	Widnes Foundry Co
Southwold	800	1900	W Jeffrey	A Fasey
***Cowes**	170	1901–2	R E Cooper	A Thorne
***Minehead**	700	1901	J J Webster	
Lowestoft	760	1902–3	D Fox	S J Trueman
Weston-super-Mare Grand	1000	1903–4	P Munroe	Mayoh & Haley
Felixtowe	2640	1905		Rogers Bros
Fleetwood	492	1910	G T Lumb	
Deal (3)	1026	1954–7	Sir W Halcrow & Partners	Concrete Piling

This list of piers is based on that contained in Simon Adamson's **Seaside Piers** published by B T Batsford Ltd in 1977. I am grateful to the author and publisher for permission to reproduce this information.

Appendix 2: Engineer's Account

'Description of a Wrought Iron Pier at Clevedon, Somerset' by John William Grover, M.Inst.C.E., a paper presented to the Institute of Civil Engineers on March 21st 1871

The original Act for constructing a wrought-iron pier at Clevedon, in Somersetshire, was obtained in the parliamentary session of 1863–64, but the works were not commenced until the autumn of 1867; little being really done upon the ground until the spring of 1868, which was singularly unpropitious for the erection of sea-structures. However, by the end of November 1868, the work was practically completed, and it has since withstood very severe storms without injury. The coast of Somersetshire is at this spot composed of dark cliffs of magnesian and mountain limestone, blocks of which, some of them in boulders of 40 tons or 50 tons in weight, lie scattered upon the beach. These are embedded in mud and slush near the shore, and amongst them lie the fragments of an ancient stone mole now completely destroyed. The site selected for the works was comparatively free from boulders and mud, being occupied by a thin promontory of rock, with a tolerably level bed from left to right, and dipping seawards at an angle of from 12° to 8°. Beyond this came a bed of soft mud, covering, at a depth of 13 feet, a substratum of hard red clay, in which boulders and stones were embedded. At the pier-head the foundation consisted of a ridge of sand, below which, at a depth of 2 feet, the bed of hard red clay was met with. The chief difficulty to be contended with was the great rise and fall of the tide, amounting at average springs to 45 feet; and the Bristol Channel being only 8 miles across at this point, the velocity of the current of the advancing or returning waters was very great, in extreme cases moving about 5½ miles in the hour. Clevedon is also exposed to the south-west, whence the prevailing winds blow up the channel. These circumstances, added to the bad holding nature of the ground, caused much delay, the stages being frequently destroyed, and the boats and barges being driven ashore and wrecked.

The structure comprises, first, an approach 180 feet long, and 20 feet wide, on a gradient of 1 in 10, the face being built of carefully squared masonry; and passing through the masonry at an angle of 45° are two mooring bolts, 2 inches in diameter, run in the rock with lead. There are also a toll-house, gates and a dwelling for the pier-master. In the next place, the body of the pier consists of eight pairs of girders, in spans of 100 feet each, having arch pieces below, the whole supported on wrought-iron piers. The girders are 3 feet 6 inches deep, and the bottom and top flanges are 18 inches wide. The girders are continuous for the entire length of the 800 feet and each girder weighs about 7 tons. The webs are of plates ⅜ths and ¼th of an inch thick; the bottom and top flanges being each composed of $\frac{9}{16}$ inch plates averaging 20 feet long, the covers being 2 feet long, $\frac{9}{16}$ths of an inch thick, and 1 foot 6 inches wide. The Vertical joints in the web are generally made with T irons, 5 inches by 2½ inches by ⅜ths of an inch and these are carried above the girders to support the planking which forms the backs of the seats, the seats themselves being carried upon the top flanges of the girders. The rivets have a uniform pitch of 6 inches and are ¾ inch in diameter. The L irons which connect the web to the bottom and top flanges are 3 inches by 3 inches by ⅜ths of an inch and are jointed by covers 2 feet long, 2½ inches by 2½ inches by ⅜ths of an inch.

The main longitudinal girders are placed at a distance of 16 feet 6 inches apart from centre to centre and are connected by transverse girders 20 feet 6 inches apart, composed of angle irons 2 inches by 2 inches by ¼th of an inch and ¼th inch webs 9 inches deep. From the ends of the transverse girders, and below the deck, run flat bars horizontally and diagonally, each bar being 3 inches by ½ inch, thus forming, with the main longitudinal girders, one large lattice girder, 16 feet 6 inches deep, laid on its side. This bracing is for the purpose of giving lateral continuity, which is also assisted by the close deck-planking, 3 inches thick, laid on joists, 10 inches by 5 inches in section, 3 feet 5 inches apart, and having a camber of 4 inches.

The piers are composed of four wrought iron piles each made of two Barlow rails, weighing 80 lbs to the yard, rivetted back to back and presenting a total section for each 100 feet span of 64 inches. These piles are built with a rake of 1 in 10 fore and aft, and they are braced together transversely by diagonal tie-rods from 18 inch to 2⅛ inches in diameter, screwed through slings at both ends; the distance pieces bring booms of four angles, iron having small cast-iron Maltese cross struts between them, fastened with ⅞ inch and 1 inch bolts. The angle irons in these booms are 3½ inches by 3½ inches by ½ inch and 4 inches by 4 inches by ½ inch, and are curved at each end to embrace the four piles. These booms are 20 feet apart on an average vertically. Sideways in elevation the piles are kept apart by T irons, 6 inches by 3 inches by ½ inch, and are braced with tie-rods from 1 inch to 1¼ inch in diameter. At the top the Barlow rails are curved to form arches longitudinally and transversely, the latter being carried round to meet each other and joined together under one strong distance girder at each pier. Longitudinally the Barlow rail arch pieces have $\frac{5}{8}$ inch plates on the backs, and the principal spandrel-piece above them is of L iron, $4\frac{1}{2}$ inches by $4\frac{1}{2}$ inches by $\frac{1}{2}$ inch, with a web plate 9 inches by $\frac{1}{2}$ inch, all being intimately connected with the web of the longitudinal girders on the top. Though the two piles on each side are separate and independent at their lower extremities, they unite and are clustered together at the top, a $\frac{1}{4}$ inch plate running up between them.

The foundations of the piles, that is, all parts below extreme low water, are formed of solid wrought-iron stems, 5 inches in diameter, shod with cast-iron screws, 2 feet in diameter; these were screwed down till a $4\frac{1}{2}$ inches rope, passing round 6 feet capstan bars, parted with the strain. They penetrate the ground to depths varying from 7 feet to 17 feet, and though made with a thread 5 inches in pitch, seldom descended more than $2\frac{1}{2}$ inches or 3 inches in a turn. The solid pile stems are connected to the Barlow rail piles by cast-iron shoes.

The iron work below extreme low-water level was coated before immersion with coal tar and naphtha; that above was painted with red lead. Where the foundations near the shore came directly upon the rock, holes were jumped, and a 4 inch wrought-iron bar was inserted and secured by a jagged key. A shoe to receive the Barlow rail was fitted and keyed on this, and the remaining space was caulked with iron cement.

The length of the longest pile was 76 feet. At extreme low water there is a depth of water of from 6 feet to 7 feet at the head, and at high-water of about 52 feet. The level of the deck above extreme high water is 16 feet, so that the height of the deck above the ground at the pier-head is about 68 feet. This is the only pier between New Passage and Land's End which commands the sea at extreme low water.

The head occupies a space of 50 feet by 40 feet and consists of one pier similar to those at intermediate distances, the others being formed with Barlow rail-piles, weighing 70 lbs to the yard, placed upright and connected together with rolled iron joists 10 feet apart vertically. There are five lower stages or decks, for landing at different states of the tide, placed 10 feet apart, and connected by stairs. The whole of the head is braced diagonally and horizontally with booms and tie-rods, so as to resist the action of the waves and the shock of steamers. It is also protected by fender piles 8 inches square, which are secured to each horizontal girder by bolts $\frac{3}{4}$ inch in diameter. It was of the greatest importance that considerable rigidity should be given to this lofty erection, exposed as it is at high tide to strong currents of water, besides the fury of the gales and the shocks from steamers, and the straining of their ropes in holding on; and not much vibration is perceptible upon it during a storm. The stairs are formed with steps rising 6 inches, and there are eleven treads; they lead to the five lower decks or landing platforms, so that the total descent is 50 feet to the lowest stage. Spaces of 2 inches are left between the battens of the steps and the stages and they are chamfered off to allow the waves to pass through. Notwithstanding these precautions, some of the steps have been carried away in a storm; and, where cost is no object, the Author would recommend in future works of this kind, that open cast-iron treads and risers should be employed.

In erecting the pier, a floating-stage was first constructed with six galvanised cylindrical corrugated iron pontoons, capable of lifting a weight of $1\frac{1}{2}$ ton each, fixed in a rectangular frame of light trellis girders, having on the top planking 3 inches thick; thus forming a deck 20 feet square, and 2 feet out of water. But, owing to the ruggedness of the shore, this stage was found inapplicable and a barge was afterwards used. This barge was 68 feet long, 14 feet beam, and decked; but it was wrecked in a gale wind of February, 1868, breaking from its moorings on the ebb tide. After drifting a distance of 5 miles, it returned on the flood, and passed within 20 feet of the pier, of which a length of 400 feet was then erected, and to which it was imprudently made fast by a rope, of $4\frac{1}{2}$ inches, which however parted with the strain. Another decked barge was then procured, and stood the weather till the pier was finished. The boats used were of the class known as whaleboats, with an air-tight compartment at each end. They were of iron and were 28 feet long, and 7 feet beam. A flat-bottomed boat was employed for launching, on account of the roughness of the beach. The first stage for screwing in the piles consisted of a framework of timber built to the proper batter both ways. A centre-rod having been fixed at 'the pier' to be commenced upon, this stage was floated out, and as the tide left, it was grounded in its proper position by a guide to the centre-rod. It was then weighted with large stones to keep it from floating away as the tide returned; the piles could then be pitched without any further setting out. As the work proceeded, and the water became deeper, a stage of driven piles was substituted. This consisted of eight piles, 5 inches by 5 inches, driven in about 6 feet; two walings were spiked on each side, 7 feet apart; on these the guides were fixed to pitch the piles, being accurately set out to the batter. The stage was braced with iron, partly for the sake of weight, and partly to diminish the area exposed to the sea. The pile being pitched, a capstan was keyed on with three steel wedges; the length of the capstan-bar was 5 feet, and the power was applied by an ordinary crab. At the periphery of the pile it required a strain of about 27 tons to turn it, or nearly 1 ton strain at the ends of the capstan-bars. The four piles composing the foundation of one pier being fixed, the next operation was to lift the pier legs into position, after they were rivetted together on the beach, and floated out by two pontoons.

Being towed into proper position at high water they were hung at one end in the tackle from a derrick or mast, 90 feet high, one pontoon being unleashed; as the tide fell the other went down, and the pier-leg was left perpendicular at low water, and ready to ship on to the connections. When the legs were fixed, and the bracing etc, put in, the pier was ready to receive the main girders. These were fixed by two methods' The first was by launching them over a span already completed; the girder was run out on rollers and being supported by a derrick, placed midway in the span, with two sets of tackle; – one holding the weight, the other being shifted back to give the necessary strain forward. This operation was found to be dangerous, and occupied three or four days for each girder. The second method was found more convenient and expeditious: thus, the girders were placed on the shore and floated out by eight pontoons, beneath their proper span; they were then lifted at one end by the derrick used to raise the piers, and at the other by a jib rigged out at the extremity of the span already completed. By this arrangement the jointing of the girder could be effected whilst it was suspended by the tackle. The pontoons were of course cut adrift before the raising was commenced.

On one occasion the whole operation, including floating the girder, took only an hour and a quarter; but this was under favourable condition of the weather; sometimes several days were employed in getting the girder into position. The number of men actually occupied in the most successful launch was fourteen, but generally thirty or forty were not sufficient. No difficulty occurred in fixing Nos 1 and 2 piers, as they were on sound rock, known locally as bastard freestone, but geologically as magnesian limestone, which in this district directly overlies the carboniferous limestone. This series overlies the coal measures with which is found the blue Pennant sandstone, a rock peculiar to this district and South Wales, and of which the abutment of the pier was built.

The raising of the derrick-pole was a matter of difficulty, the surface of the lower beach being chiefly mud. It was first put up with an anchor weighing over 6 cwt., on each of the two broadside guys, the other two guys, fore and aft, being made fast to the work; but as the tide grew strong one anchor dragged, and let the derrick down. Two anchors, weighing 6 cwt each were then tried, with wooden piles driven against their flukes, but this was of no avail; finally, large pieces of rock were floated out to the proper position, and then sunk; and to these the guys were attached by a chain, fixed to a ring-bolt.

No 5 span and No 5 pier were built in ten days; but the entire work took fifteen months; in some cases as many as three months per span, when the weather was unfavourable. The average number of men employed was about sixty.

The metal in the girders was calculated to bear tensile and compressive strains of 5 tons per square inch. The strain on the piles in compression was 2 tons per square inch when wholly loaded.

The structure is made to carry 1 cwt to the superficial foot of available deck surface, being 16 cwt per foot run, or 80 tons per span of 100 feet. Specimens of all the iron employed were carefully tested at the works; and one span of the completed structure was loaded in the centre with 42 tons of stone, placed in such a manner as to be equal to a distributed load of 80 tons on the span, exclusive of its own weight. The deflection in the centre with this weight was $1\frac{1}{4}$ inch, the calculated deflection being 1 inch, and it was only temporary. The mean permanent set being about $\frac{2}{5}$ths of an inch. The weight of wrought iron was under 370 tons, and of cast iron 7 tons; and the entire cost of the works was under £10,000.

The contractors for the pier were Hamilton's Windsor Ironworks Company of Liverpool and for the approaches Mr Ambrose Oliver of Hitcham. The works were designed and carried out by Mr R J Ward, M.Inst.C.E. and the Author of the Paper, as joint Engineers; Mr J Wallace Peggs being the resident Engineer.

Appendix 3: Quotations

"Clevedon's appeal is largely because of its many charming examples of Victorian building and planting. One of its greatest attractions is its Victorian Pier. . . Long live Clevedon as a complete town which it would not be if it ever lost its pier.
John Betjeman, March 28th 1969

"Clevedon Pier is a unique and elegant construction. . . . For over a hundred years it has been a landmark on this beautiful coast, and the pivot of a lovely town . . ."
Country Life, September 2nd 1971

". . . the simplicity and straightforward approach of its pier sums up the whole environment of Clevedon."
The Architectural Review, May 1969

"This is undoubtedly the most graceful pier in the country."
Report to the Victorian Society on remaining Seaside Piers by Simon Adamson (reproduced in his book *Seaside Piers* 1977)

"Clevedon Pier is a wonderful piece of Victorian engineering and Victorian town planning. Striding boldly out into the Severn Estuary, it dominates and enhances a seascape and landscape of the utmost distinction."
Sir Arthur Elton, *Engineering*, July 1971

"From the further studies carried out, and detailed later in this report it is considered that it would be feasible, from an engineering standpoint, to restore the pier to a state compatible with its appearance over the period 1900-1910."
Engineer's Report to Clevedon Pier Preservation Trust by Peter Mason, May 18th 1979

"Clevedon Pier is a fine example of early wrought iron work . . . it is a thing of beauty that harmonises with and enhances its environment. The pier has outlived its commercial usefulness but it is an asset in the same way that a park is an asset, and in the same way it needs money and proper attention to maintain it."
Engineering, July 1971

"Clevedon without a Pier would be like a dog without a tail."
Rev. Charles Marson, Vicar of St Andrew's, Clevedon 1913

"Clevedon Pier is a structure of national importance."
Mrs E Fawcett, Secretary of the Victorian Society 1970

"It is a fit companion to the Clifton Suspension Bridge, six years its senior, spanning the Gorge with similar confidence and strength, and their more distant neighbour, the Royal Albert Bridge at Saltash. Clevedon's Pier could be a cruel reminder that we are wantonly careless of our monuments to the daring and inventiveness of English engineers. The Crumlin Viaduct and Brunel's great wrought iron span over the Wye are already gone."
Press release by the Clevedon Pier Restoration Committee, July 1971

"Its structure is a delight, and it has been rated one of the top three piers in the country by the Department of the Environment."
Avon Conservation News, pub. 1979, Avon County Council

". . . one of the finest examples of the seaside pier."
The Architects' Journal, September 24th 1975

"Clevedon is of national importance. Its charming centre is agreeable and prosperous, and its setting incomparable. It offers the best of the Victorian age and its conservation is urgently necessary."
Country Life, October 2nd 1975

"I think the most beautiful pleasure piers on the coasts of England are the West Pier at Brighton and its elegant outline and Clevedon Pier, Somerset which looks like a Whistler oil sketch or a Japanese print."
John Betjeman, December 1979

"One of the most visually pleasing of the 84 seaside piers which were built around the British coast."
W K V Gale, Consultant to DOE on Iron and Steel History, 1978

"I think Clevedon Pier is perhaps the most beautiful pier in the country . . ."
Roy Worskett, Bath City Architect

"of the 55 remaining piers reviewed . . . three piers, Bangor, Brighton West and Clevedon, were recommended as worthy of Grade I listing."
CBA Advisory Panel on Industrial Monuments, June 13th 1975

". . . its future ought to be decided on environmental grounds, not on narrowly economic ones."
The Architectural Review, December 1970

"Gavin Henderson (author of a forth-coming book on seaside piers) is adamant that, whatever the likely fate of the majority of our remaining 40 piers, we should make every effort to preserve at least three: Brighton's two piers as well as the one at Clevedon in Somerset."
The Guardian, February 28th 1975

"probably the best Victorian pier in Britain."

Ian Nairn, *The Sunday Times*, August 29th 1971

"If anything is worth preserving it is Clevedon pier and it needs to be taken very seriously indeed . . . I do not know of any other example of this type of construction in our part of England. It is a most important monument for the South West to retain, and it is one of the artefacts of a great period of expansion. The pier is a most distinguished ornament and an essential feature of Clevedon as it was conceived and developed."

Dr R A Buchanan, Director of the Centre for the Study of the History of Technology, February 1971

'A new era in Clevedon has commenced. The light has at last broken upon us. The pier will be the completion of beautiful Clevedon."

Clevedon Mercury, February 23rd 1867

"There are those who are prepared to buy it as old iron and carry it away, a proceeding which would be a terrible eyesore and a terrible shame for Clevedon."

Eustace Button, August 16th 1890

"Not only is it a neat example of early industrial wrought ironwork, but the pier is a major Victorian element in a town which has notably preserved its Victorian area."

The Architects' Journal, November 24th 1970

Bibliography

LOCAL GUIDES

Rutter J. **The Clevedon Guide,** 1829

Chilcott's Clevedon New Guide, 7th Edition, Bristol 1856

Short R S. **The Complete Guide to Clevedon,** circa 1880

The Royal Cabinet Album of Clevedon, circa 1880

Visitors Handbook to Clevedon, 1890

Mercury & Courier **Clevedonia,** 1892

Whitby, R. **Mates Illustrated Clevedon,** Bournemouth 1903

ARTICLES/PAPERS

Clevedon Pier **Engineering,** December 6th 1867

Grover, J W. 'Description of a Wrought Iron Pier at Clevedon, Somerset', **Proceedings of the Institute of Civil Engineers** Vol XXXII 1871 (see Appendix 2) Mathematical analysis pp 171–91 of the same volume

Rayner, J., Mallory, K. 'Clevedon Pier' pp 325–28 **The Architectural Review,** May 1969

Phillips, M. 'Clevedon Pier is falling down' pp 434–5 **Engineering,** July 1971

Elton, M A. 'The Road to Clevedon Pier' pp 568–571 **Country Life,** September 2nd 1971

Lee, E T. Engineer's Report to the Leisure Services Committee, Woodspring District Council, November 7th 1974

Bradley, M. 'The Pleasures of Piers' pp 606–636 **The Architects' Journal,** September 24th 1975

Curl, J S. 'A Victorian Coastal Arcadia' pp 830–32 **Country Life,** October 2nd 1975

Gale W K V. 'The Sad Decay of Clevedon Pier' pp 50–3 **Building Conservation,** Winter 1978

Mason, P. Engineer's Report on Clevedon Pier to Clevedon Pier Preservation Trust, May 18th 1979

BOOKS

Sheppard, R. **Cast Iron in Building,** 1945

Pevsner, *N.* **Pioneers of Modern Design,** Penguin 1964

Trevelyan, *G M.* **Illustrated English Social History,** repub. Pelican 1964

Davis, *T.* **John Nash,** 1966

Hern, *A.* **The Seaside Holiday,** London 1967

Rayner, *J.*, *Mallory*, *K.* **Clevedon Pier, Somerset,** Building Study (unpub.) London 1967

Lindley, *K.* **Seaside Architecture,** pub. Hugh Evelyn London 1973

Adamson, *S H.* **Seaside Piers,** pub. Batsford London 1977

Illustrations

All other illustrations
are the copyright of the author